D0759929

NATIVE
AMERICAN
NATIONS

Apache

F.A. BIRD

CONTENT CONSULTANT: CHANCE L. LANDRY

**Checkerboard
Library**

An Imprint of Abdo Publishing
abdobooks.com

ABDOBOOKS.COM

Published by Abdo Publishing, a division of ABDO, PO Box 398166, Minneapolis, Minnesota 55439.
Copyright © 2022 by Abdo Consulting Group, Inc. International copyrights reserved in all countries.
No part of this book may be reproduced in any form without written permission from the publisher.
Checkerboard Library™ is a trademark and logo of Abdo Publishing.

Printed in the United States of America, North Mankato, Minnesota
102021
012022

THIS BOOK CONTAINS
RECYCLED MATERIALS

Design and Production: Mighty Media, Inc.
Editor: Liz Salzmann
Cover Photograph: Angela Hampton Picture Library/Alamy Photo
Interior Photographs: Ad_hominem/Shutterstock Images, p. 7; Denver Public Library Special
    Collections, p. 25; Everett Collection/Shutterstock Images, p. 27; Grand Canyon National Park/Flickr,
    pp. 13, 19, 29; kojihirano/Shutterstock Images, p. 21; LHBLLC/Shutterstock Images, p. 5; Library of
    Congress, p. 23; Midnight Believer/Flickr, p. 9; mphillips007/iStockphoto, p. 11; University of Southern
    California Libraries, pp. 15, 17

Library of Congress Control Number: 2021943038

Publisher's Cataloging-in-Publication Data
Names: Bird, F.A., author.
Title: Apache / by F.A. Bird
Description: Minneapolis, Minnesota : Abdo Publishing, 2022 | Series: Native American nations | Includes
    online resources and index.
Identifiers: ISBN 9781532197154 (lib. bdg.) | ISBN 9781098219284 (ebook)
Subjects: LCSH: Apache Indians--Juvenile literature. | Indians of North America--Juvenile literature. |
    Indigenous peoples--Social life and customs--Juvenile literature. | Cultural anthropology--Juvenile
    literature.
Classification: DDC 973.0497--dc23

Contents

CHAPTER 1

Homelands

The Apache moved from northern Canada to their new desert homeland around 1200 CE. The Apache settled in the deserts, plains, and mountains of the Southwest.

The Apache name comes from a Zuni word meaning "the Enemy." Early Spanish colonists used this name for all people who spoke the Athabaskan language. But each tribe of Athabaskan-speaking people has its own preferred name.

One of the larger tribes was the Jicarilla. They lived in northeastern New Mexico. The Mescalero lived in western Texas and southeastern New Mexico. The Mimbreños lived in southwestern New Mexico. The Chiricahua lived in southern Arizona and northern Mexico. The Dilzhe'e (Tonto), Aravaipa, and Coyotero lived in central and eastern Arizona. The Lipan lived in Mexico, Texas, and Oklahoma.

The Apache homelands included the Salt River Canyon in Arizona.

CHAPTER 2

Society

The main social unit of the Apache was the family group. It was important for everyone to work together and share in all things. This ensured the health and well-being of all members.

A **band** was made up of two to five families with a total of ten to fifty people. Each band had a leader, who could be a man or a woman. By example, the leader reminded everyone of their duty to the family and their band's traditions.

People could not marry within their own band. When a couple got married, they lived with the woman's mother's band. This created family ties between the bands. A group of related bands formed a tribe.

THE APACHE HOMELANDS

WASHINGTON

OREGON

MONTANA

IDAHO

WYOMING

NEVADA

UTAH

CALIFORNIA

NORTH DAKOTA

SOUTH DAKOTA

NEBRASKA

COLORADO

KANSAS

MINNESOTA

WISCONSIN

IOWA

MICHIGAN

ILLINOIS

INDIANA

OHIO

MISSOURI

KENTUCKY

WEST VIRGINIA

VIRGINIA

NEW YORK

PENNSYLVANIA

MAINE

VERMONT

NEW HAMPSHIRE

MASSACHUSETTS

RHODE ISLAND

CONNECTICUT

NEW JERSEY

DELAWARE

MARYLAND

WASHINGTON, DC

ARIZONA

Dilzhe'e

Aravaipa

Coyotero

Chiricahua

NEW MEXICO

Mimbreños

Mescalero

Jicarilla

OKLAHOMA

Lipan

ARKANSAS

TENNESSEE

NORTH CAROLINA

SOUTH CAROLINA

TEXAS

Lipan

MEXICO

Lipan

MISSISSIPPI

ALABAMA

GEORGIA

LOUISIANA

FLORIDA

N W E S

THE APACHE HOMELANDS

CHAPTER 3

Homes

A **common type of home was a grass and brush house called a *wickiup* (WIH-kee-uhp).** To build a *wickiup*, the Apache set four saplings in the ground. The saplings were tied together at the top to make a sturdy frame. Next, more saplings were spaced around the base of the circle. These were then bent in an arc and tied to the other saplings for support.

To make the roof, yucca leaf fibers were made into cord. The cord was stitched around the *wickiup* in bundles from the bottom up. A small hole was left in the top of the *wickiup* to let smoke out. Buffalo or deer hide was sometimes used to cover the sides of the *wickiup*, especially in the winter months.

A *wickiup*'s doorway always faced east to greet the morning sun.

CHAPTER 4

Food

There was little rain each year in the Apache homelands. But the Apache were experts at surviving on the desert's few resources. Apache women collected acorns, seeds, cactus fruit, and other plants for food and medicine. Some Apache had gardens with corn, melons, and pumpkins.

A **band** established different camps to follow game. These camps were near water and were used year after year. The Apache hunted buffalo, elk, deer, rabbits, and birds, including turkey. They also ate fish.

When the Spanish came to explore the Americas, they moved onto Apache lands and took over their hunting grounds. This made it hard for the Apache to get enough food. So, they **raided** Spanish settlements for cattle and other supplies that had been taken from them.

A mule deer in Great Sand Dunes National Park, part of the Apache homelands

CHAPTER 5

Clothing

Apache clothing varied based on the weather. They wore **tanned** deerskin clothes when it was cold. They wore cotton clothes when it was warm.

Women wore wraparound skirts. They also wore simple **ponchos** as shirts. The men wore **breechcloths**, buckskin leggings, and shirts decorated with beads. And they carried blankets and Mexican **serapes** (suh-RAH-pee). Both men and women wore deerskin shawls.

The Apache were famous for their knee-high buckskin boots. The boots were often decorated with **fringe** or silver **conchos**. The Apache traded boots with their neighbors for things such as salt and blankets. When the Europeans came, the Apache traded with them for guns.

Apache clothes were often decorated with long fringe.

CHAPTER 6

Crafts

Apache women carried all of their families' possessions in baskets. These baskets could be woven from the shoots of desert shrubs and young trees, ponderosa pine needles, or cattails. A basket that carried water was called a *tus*.

A *tus* was made from willow and cottonwood shoots. In the spring, these shoots were cut in sections. These sections were cut lengthwise into three pieces. Then, they were woven together to make the bottom of the *tus*.

The woven pieces were coiled to form the outside shape of the *tus*. The coils were sewn tightly together with yucca plant strips. To make the baskets watertight, they were brushed with melted piñon tree sap. The sap hardened like a **varnish** and sealed the *tus*.

Girls learned basket weaving and other crafts by watching their mothers and grandmothers.

CHAPTER 7

Family

When a man and a woman wanted to get married, they would live together away from the family for two weeks. When they came back, they were considered married.

The groom moved to the bride's mother's family camp. He brought food for everyone to share. But he was forbidden to ever speak to his mother-in-law. Eye contact between them was considered bad manners.

Children were always welcome and loved in an Apache home. Orphans were taken in by new families and raised as sons and daughters. Apache children were trained from an early age to be mentally tough and physically **disciplined**. Boys were taught to hunt by their fathers and uncles.

Apache grandmothers often helped raise their grandchildren.

CHAPTER 8

Children

Apache babies were carried on their mothers' backs while bundled on a **cradleboard**. The cradleboard was often hung in a tree near the home. This way, the baby could watch the family's daily activities. When the baby was old enough to walk, he or she helped the mother gather wood, water, and food.

Girls continued to help their mothers throughout their entire lives. Apache parents rarely punished their children. And they taught them to respect elders as knowledgeable, treasured members of society.

Apache children learn traditional music and dancing.

CHAPTER 9
Traditions

Some Apache do not speak the name of a dead relative for at least a year. They believe the dead person is on a new journey and needs the time to adjust. At the end of the year, there is a ceremony to call the ancestors to take the dead person to the afterlife. The Apache call this the Land of Forever Summer.

Like many Native Americans, the Apache consider owls bad luck and messengers of bad news. They do not tell jokes or stories about owls. It is bad luck to even talk about them. The Apache believe that the ghosts of dead people live in owls. The dead speak to the living through the owl's hoots and cries.

The Apache consider it bad luck to hear an owl hooting nearby.

CHAPTER 10

War

When the Europeans arrived, the Apache became warriors to protect their lands and way of life. An Apache warrior party could travel up to 70 miles (13 km) a day. They were experts at hiding, tracking, and leaving no sign of their passing. Because they traveled in small groups, the Apache avoided big battles. Instead, they fought in a hit-and-run style.

During a **raid**, the Apache slipped silently into a settlement and took what they needed to replace what was taken from them. If a member of the party was killed, his friends and family had the duty to take **revenge**.

Apache warrior parties were usually made up of four to twelve men.

CHAPTER II

Contact with Europeans

In the 1600s, the Spanish stole Apache land and built settlements there. This invasion led to **retaliation** missions by the Apache. In 1848, the United States won a war with Mexico and took control of the Apache lands.

In 1861, an Apache **raiding** party drove off cattle belonging to a white rancher. It also kidnapped a **ranch hand's** child. An Apache man named Cochise was wrongfully accused of the act. He and his relatives were arrested.

Cochise escaped. But his relatives were hanged. This started a 25-year war with the United States. Thousands of Apaches and hundreds of settlers died. Cochise did not surrender until the Chiricahua **Reservation** was formed in 1872. He died there June 8, 1874. Then, the rest of the Apache people were sent to different reservations.

During the 1800s, the US government forced many Apache families to send their children away to boarding schools. Students at the schools were often mistreated.

CHAPTER 12

Geronimo

Geronimo was the last of the great Apache leaders. He was born in 1823 near the Gila River in present-day Arizona. He was a member of the Bedonkohe **band** of the Chiricahua Apache tribe.

Geronimo became an important leader during the 25-year war with the United States. When Cochise died in 1874, Geronimo refused to surrender and live on a **reservation**. He continued to fight against the US Army until September 1886.

Geronimo and the surviving members of his band were sent to reservations. Geronimo died on February 17, 1909, at Fort Sill, Oklahoma. He is buried with many of his Chiricahua people.

Geronimo's Chiricahua name was *Goyathlay*, which means "one who yawns." Mexican soldiers gave him the name Geronimo.

CHAPTER 13

The Apache Today

Today, some Athabaskan-speaking people live in towns and cities. Others live on **reservations**. There are Apache reservations in Arizona, New Mexico, and Oklahoma. These reservations cover almost 4.5 million acres (1.8 million ha).

Many Apache reservations have museums and **cultural** centers. These places help preserve and teach people about Apache culture. Visitors can also see old forts and other historic sites.

The Athabaskan-speaking people are working to preserve their culture. Many also make important contributions in fields such as medicine, law, business, and education.

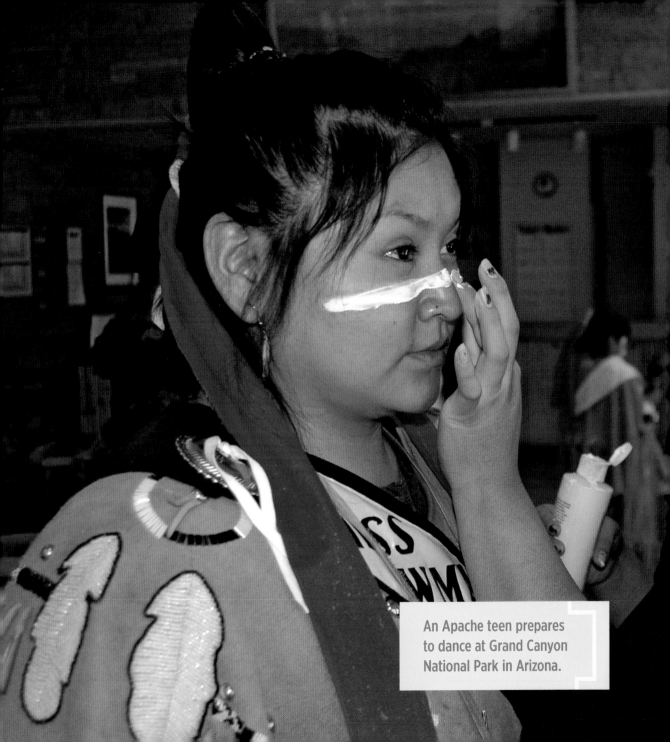

An Apache teen prepares to dance at Grand Canyon National Park in Arizona.

Glossary

band—a number of persons acting together; a subgroup of a tribe.

breechcloth—a piece of cloth, usually worn by men. It wraps between the legs and around the waist.

concho—a round, flat piece of silver jewelry, often strung together and decorated with turquoise.

cradleboard—a decorated flat board with a wooden band at the top that protects the baby's head.

culture—the customs, arts, and tools of a nation or people at a certain time. Something related to culture is cultural.

disciplined—developed and trained by instruction and exercise.

fringe—a border or trim made of threads or cords, either loose or tied together in small bunches.

poncho—a large piece of cloth or other material with a slit in the middle for the head to go through.

raid—a sudden attack.

ranch hand—a person hired to work on a ranch.

reservation—a piece of land set aside by the government for Native Americans to live on.

retaliation—an instance of getting revenge for a wrong or injury.

revenge—harm done in return for a wrong.

serape—an outer garment like a cloak or poncho, often brightly colored and worn by men.

tanned—having been made into leather by being soaked in a special liquid.

varnish—a liquid that gives a smooth, glossy appearance to wood.

ONLINE RESOURCES

Booklinks
NONFICTION NETWORK
FREE! ONLINE NONFICTION RESOURCES

To learn more about the Apache, please visit **abdobooklinks.com** or scan this QR code. These links are routinely monitored and updated to provide the most current information available.

Index